To The House Ghost

Books by Paula Rankin

By the Wreckmaster's Cottage
Augers
To the House Ghost

To The House Ghost

Paula Rankin

Carnegie-Mellon University Press
Pittsburgh 1985

ACKNOWLEDGEMENTS

Some of these poems have appeared in the following magazines:
Agni Review: "We Never Get to the End of it All;" *The American Poetry Review:* "Leftovers," "Middle Age;" *Crazy Horse:* "To the House Ghost;" *Louisville Review:* "Being Refused Local Credit," "The New Tenants in Our Old Duplex," "Not Meeting;" *New Jersey Poetry Review:* "Two Ways of Listening to Rain;" *Memphis State Poetry Review:* "Stigmata;" *Missouri Review:* "Webs," "Glossolalia;" *Poetry Miscellany:* "Poem Using Unused Lines;" *Poetry Northwestern:* "Unreasonable Footprints;" *Quarterly West:* "Somewhere Else;" *South Carolina Review:* "The Red Shoe;" *Tar River Poetry:* "Goldfinches at the Nuclear Plant;" *Tendril:* "Making Tracks;" *Three Rivers Poetry Journal:* "A Poem for Spring;" *Vanderbilt Poetry Review:* "Preservatives," "Sadness and Fingernails;" *Woman Poet: The South,* ed. by Dara Wier: "Here."

The publication of this book is supported by grants from the National Endowment for the Arts in Washington, D.C., a Federal agency, and from the Pennsylvania Council on the Arts.

Library of Congress Catalog Number 84-72993
ISBN 0-88748-013-6
ISBN 0-88748-014-4 Pbk.
Copyright © 1985 by Paula Rankin
Printed and bound in the United States of America
First Edition

CONTENTS

I

WE NEVER GET TO THE END OF IT ALL

Even when I think we're at the end,
crates of clothes and mementos packed,
there is still my great-grandmother
laid out in the tintype,
hands folded across the bosom
of her Sunday dress, waiting
for her likeness. Ahead there's a man
with his head inside a black curtain,
flashing a pan of light. Off to the side,
my grandmother, twelve, is wooed
by a muslin apron, its deep pockets
where the hands, shirking burdens, might hide.
Air stalls for its moment
and passes, like the child's dream
of being a child. The man packs his equipment
in saddledbags and rides off.
My grandmother sits by the bed all day,
all night. Later she will place the tintype
face down in her lap, scratching a nail's vow
into metal: *I will never have a child.*

THE NEW TENANTS IN OUR OLD DUPLEX

In the garage, over their car,
swallows' nests drip
spittle and a paste of weeds, twigs,
droppings; upstairs, by their bedroom
window, a pair of starlings line a mud cup
in the box air-conditioner,
and all morning it sounds
like boiled eggs
popping, after the water's run
out, the pot's still on the burner
on high.

If he shaves by the bathroom mirror
he shaves lips, ears,
eyesight. She combs long undulations
of face.

And the phone rings once or twice
for Rankin, they don't live here.
Or sometimes it rings
and no one asks for anyone.
Who's this? Who's this? Who's this?

Their dog finds new times
for barking, new reasons.

PRESERVATIVES

The night the ocean froze in Virginia
we walked with lanterns
on top of the breakers, listening in disbelief
to the silence. I knelt,
searched for fish and periwinkles
embedded at split moments of turning;
you found bird tracks pricked
on the swell of a wave.

How I loved you.
I thought of ferns on fossilized slate,
of people packed in storage
until a later century's
necessary miracle of scientists
who'd chip them out,
teaching unimaginable transitions.

Above us, winter birds, crying *hurry, hurry,*
flocked further south.

Six years, and I taste salt
when I shake you over memory.

Some nights I cry out your name
through trees, toward sky,
and the wind comes behind,
sweeping. It doesn't know what to do
when it meets you: it thinks of a bird,
a leaf, a compromise with all the shapes
that shape it. Then it remembers.
No; I am the wind.

11

WEBS

By September, we cannot move through the yard
without tearing whole networks
of tracery down.
It's been a long time since I've been trapped
by lies this intricate and silken,
and I lie down in the grass
to see if it's all really spun from one's body
like angel hair, each careful knot
an alibi shot with sunlight—
the spinner paused here, here, and here.

My grandmother was married
forever. She took her broom
and swept clothesline, trees, and house
free of spiders' and hearts' entanglements.
She whisked great plans
from the veins of leaves and children.
She moistened thread on the tip of her tongue
and sewed sleeves back onto shoulders
and died mistrusting anyone's account
of whereabouts.

TO THE HOUSE GHOST

Just because I turn on the light
it doesn't mean I don't want you around.
I know how you like to keep your own
shredded space among hangers and vents;
you think I have no room for you
at the table or in bed. But listen:
I have made room in my ribcage more than once.
There is always something that wants to move over
to borrow air like trouble.

You could light my cigarettes.
After I'm in bed, lean over my impossible wishes
and blow them out. Lie down and tell me
who cut you down in your prime,
describe the weapon.

VISITATIONS

Lying in bed at 4:30 A.M.,
I watch night lift from the trees,
their edges defining themselves
like people who have everything they need.

This would be a good time to call
all the people in my other lives:
it's 2:30 in Salt Lake and Seattle,
5:30 in Cambridge, not late
for anyone I love. I have heard
that even the dead answer their phones
if you dial and hold and pray.

I want Love to come down from the trees
with all its arms and legs and mouths
saying, I lied, I don't have everything I need.

LEFTOVERS

When the mind thinks of leaving,
suddenly the good things rise
like calm, communicative children
misplaced in a classroom
of autistics. How we love them,
dragging their patches of light
across our yard. How we stare
at these children
who enter all our metaphors,
each one lit with his aura of lostness,
each one flaring for his moment
in memory, saying, *Wait, this signifies.*

And there is the non-metaphorical child
whose coffin was dug up,
ten years in the ground,
and still there was something,
something to dust.

STIGMATA

". . .many genuine and devout recipients
would conceal them, or pray that they might
suffer the pain but show no outward sign of
the wound to excite the curious."
—*Phenomena: A Book of Wonders*

More than the saint
who fasted
for a cross
to come slashing its love
for his hand
are those whose irises burn
in least light,
whose eardrums collapse
at a whisper.

More than those who pray in public
are those who appear to be shaking
only from cold, who ask
for a closet.

Something wants to describe
itself on skin, to explain
why the bleeding heart is,
must be. Something else
dreads attention, hiding
in a rash
beneath a wedding band,
under eyelids.

There are more
who are quiet.
Many more
who are very quiet.

THE RED SHOE

I first saw it
mashing centipede
on the safety island
at a time in my life
when I was trying to hold
too many bodies
together, under too many roofs.
Its patent, cracked, bounced
the sunlight and me
into the story of the cure
for the girl who loved dancing
all night in red shoes:
I felt for pieces of charred foot
in its lining.

There are no immaculate
getaways. But in that moment
I dreamed a shoe
in a dead break and run
miles ahead, slapping itself clean
of mud and seedlings; I dreamed a runner,
of two minds about it,
who had carefully unbuckled one shoe
and left it tamping the earth
beneath a traffic light's split-second arrows.

It got to be like a friend
a place to go stand
on one leg
and practice balance.
I kept asking for which of desire's worlds
it served as a sign,

the one we can't see
or the one we can.
One had a runner in it.
The other sat on an island
patiently filling with seasons.
In Spring there were mud
and maple wings. In July, sorrel
and mullein. In Fall, leaf mulch
and lichen. By December
it was turning into snow.

UNREASONABLE FOOTPRINTS

Sometimes we wake to a yard of them,
scars gouged deep in mud
as barrow pits, reminders of how much circles,
walks up to have a look
without letting us know.

Then the inevitable lantern and hound,
nights we stalk these fields with neighbors
to flush the mystery, to fill holes with an eyewitness account,
to come back with a name for the vanished,
something with fur, real blood, a scent.

I never tell you how I love the not knowing,
those moments when we wallow in our ignorance
and the trespasser is anything it needs to be
to get attention. I like to think it's the Possibility
for love, puzzling the moves it should make,

not knowing enough
to come in out of the rain. Or these auras
of absences our bodies are said to emanate:
I like to think the vanished go on inside them,
that above "Goodbye" hovers a print whose owner

even air cannot help but shape itself around.
Most of all I think of entering that moment
before the foot, poised over all possible tracks,
begins to come down, before desire chooses
its avenue to memory through us,

harrowing the darkness between like clods of warm earth.

SOMEWHERE ELSE

The waitress
takes our order, but clearly
her mind is
          somewhere else —

It's one of those days,
she says, handing us drinks
for someone else's thirst
which we forgive, though even our forgiveness
interrupts a conversation
                    somewhere else —

Our roast burns
for a man across town,
a thankless child,
bad luck, no money,
customers full of unlikelihoods
here, possibilities
there —

And in our children's eyes
we see the meal we've bought them
go cold, so impatient are they
to be already
where they're going,
spinning rubber down a driveway
where houselights are just beginning to come on,
it's just beginning to be dark.

BEING REFUSED LOCAL CREDIT

Too new in town, we're told,
though we give twenty years
of references, debts owed
and paid, companies that begged
us as risks. How long does it take,
I ask, am told, Years.
OK, I shrug to my husband; so we'll pay cash.
But my heart's not in it,
knowing how everything it ever wanted arrived
before the wherewithal,
how without the foolhardy trust
of certain friends and strangers
I'd have had nothing, nothing.

This may be the town I'll learn
to be good in, filled with counters, aisles
where my credit's no good and my hands
stay in my pockets, counting costs.

Suddenly we don't need
almost everything. For years
we're too new
to be trusted; We're back
in those barracks-turned-apartments
before our first child:
We're reading *1984* in paperback, taking turns

reading aloud the passages that seem most possible,
war and loneliness and rats.
The daughter we can't pay for
takes all this in, with our screams and yelling and rock
    music;
the tiny clot of heart muscles contracts,
perusing. . . .

You're working overtime,
not enough. If it's day shift
I sweep, huge-bellied, where I can,
visit the woman next door
who seems to me so wise
with grown children.
If third shift, I bolt-lock the doors,
sit up half the night
with a butcher knife
as you told me, asking
Who would want to steal from us? Who?

MIDDLE AGE

The groundhog we dumped in the woods
is back in the yard
where he lies with his head in a cloud
of lice, an aura of flies,
a pale apple-green shimmering.

You say the dogs bring him back,
wanting praise, claiming credit.
At first I thought him but one more proof
of Spring, like wasps in vents,
ticks in children. All I know is he's there
when I walk to the mailbox,
when I lie in the sun,
when I look up at the stars
to say we're all nearer
to each other than we are.

He's a message from my father,
refusing to settle with the dead,
warning me I lack the skills
to keep them buried. Something's trying
to keep me from grief, but I'm not fooled:
love doesn't come back
like this, nor second chance.

Children gather to poke the remains,
then go fishing. I'm left
where the dead and the young
would keep me, cleaning up the mess.
What a mess they leave.

TWO WAYS OF LISTENING TO RAIN

That April morning, the sycamore had opened its leaves
like plates, it wanted rain so. We opened our mouths
like bowls, wanting what we could not name,
the tongue newly afloat in its silver
inarticulation. Tonight a steady rain
has fallen for hours, pestling my yard
with fallen leaves; walking through the certainties
of mulch, I can steady my tongue
to say backwards, Ah, yes, regeneration!
We wanted to live again! To know, through our palms,
how leaves must rush at their first green shock
of chlorophyll. Lonely man, I think I hear you
alone in your tower, listening to rain,
saying it's time for the dead
to bury the dead. I think I hear
you saying the butter-yellow maple
is drained and umbered
from what you remember. You speak
of diminishing,
having learned nothing from seasons and their selfish,
magnificent gestures: It's my turn, they say, Move over.
I hear them in this rain
on slick paths of leaves
where balance begins
and the wind sounds like water rushing
inside tree trunks
or inside wrists
if we could hear ourselves
pounding.

TENNESSEE WEDDING

They are seventeen. The preacher
tells them "tonight at 6:30." We rush
to Kroger's for a cake
with two tiny figurines
sunk to their shins in frosting
and white plastic bells, to the florist
for a yellow rosebud bouquet,
to the liquor store three counties away
for champagne, to their trailer
with chairs, a bassinette, table, mattress,
dishes. Without us, there would be no pay
for the preacher, no asking
who gives this woman, does anyone know
just cause, no hole cut in a glove
for a ring. There would be only
a field of weeds, tires,
carburetors, a trailer
among two dozen other trailers
in each of which three or four families
sleep, eat, love
which sometimes leads
to shooting each other
or blowing holes through trailer walls
or frying dog food
or kicking each other out
to sleep on the frozen mud all night
with loose dogs or leaving
for good. Without us, no flowers,
no mustaches
of blancmange, no gulping
of spirits. Only a field.
Trailers. Eyes
in which a fearful, awful love,
like a caught breath, saves
everything we are up to this moment.

WHEN THE FAT WOMAN THINS

My husband says
she'll leave her husband,
as though obesity were goodness,
straining no one's heart
but the bearer's, as though beauty
which is more than resignation
(when we turn with a sigh
from our bodies and try to believe
in our inner loveliness, depth)
were only a gesture of rhetoric,
the epidictic, show-off kind, —
all pleasure, no instruction.

But to me she's a wonder,
pushing back from our tables,
saying *no,* and *No.*
Even as I write this
she backs out my driveway
on less, in less, all glittery surface
and sleekness of neck.

Oh what has become of her
pretty face, and all her deep
resources? Somewhere out there,
does cellulite crimp air
like wrinkles, does melted fat
undulate through waves of gravity?
And if the air we breathe
seems sometimes thick, heavy,
does it mean someone must pay,
someone must inhale
another's losses?

Let us believe
in her change-for-the-better,
let us swear by what seems the sudden
jutting of cheek and collar bones.
It seems overnight
but took years, perhaps her whole life
to count down to this.

II

SADNESS AND FINGERNAILS

"There have been cases of men and women who were so embarrassed by age spots on their hands, they wore gloves to serve dinner to guests."—from an advertisement for Esoterica cream.

It's true the hands know too much
and show it, having picked their way
through songs, greeting cards, poems
to the truth about those with us
in spirit: they're gone,
the fingers report,
back from their ferreting excursions,
their tips blue with cold.
Small wonder we learn
to stop asking them
where they've been
or what it's like out there on the airy edge
of trouble and hope.

My mother calls hers back in like troops
from the Siberian front, like children.

Then comes the sadness of her fingernails,
bone meal pale as oyster shells
with their scoops
of sand and emptiness. Then comes her daily
manicure, hours lost between filings, layers
of polish and gloss.

And what are we going to do if it turns out
this was our only life
when it's clear we're denied the right number
of fingers, not enough for counting
all the losses of faces
from memory, not enough to touch
all the people we love,

not enough to play the piano
the way we've always wanted it played,
Maple Leaf Rag with undertones of Wagner —
and too many fingers to take apart the innards
of quartz crystal watches, asking
What makes you tick? and too many
for one
gold
ring,
and not enough to chew our way to calm
or flash lacquers at the dead
like caution lights.

And what if the past
inherits us,
the past whose fingernails keep growing.
extending the distance, nudging us away?

My mother paints her nails:
Peachpetal frost, Snowberry, Crystal Ice.
And the hours and days
drift through her fingers
like ghosts,
gloved in a fog
of myth, a gauze of memory, floating
like wafted breath through gaps in
blowing on her fingernails to dry.

HERE

For the first time
I pull your death up
onto paper and write
bullet through the lung.
It was our first Sunday night
in the new house, my first
a thousand miles from you.
My husband had bought a grate,
screen, tongs, hearth-broom, ash-shovel,
bellows to keep air
burning. Watching him, watching fire,
I let myself feel
I'd moved far enough
to be good. The phone rang.
A voice told me
of an accident, a gun
not even meant for you.
The voice had held you last,
it had last cradled your head in its hands,
and I didn't recognize it.

I had to pretend it was
nothing. I remember going down
steep, dark stairs
to the basement to put a load
in the dryer. I remember
the washing machine's chipped lid
as it held me up
with both hands, my mouth
opening and closing, something
refusing to rise from the well

behind my molars, my throat
like a sink drain clogged with hair
and dental floss.

My second feeling: *Traitor,* you've left me
the whole burden of memory.

I read Proust for a year, starring
every other paragraph, writing
Amens in the margins. I remember thinking,
maybe he's right,
maybe five years down the road
I'll be someone I barely know,
full of fresh brain and skin cells,
all the zillions
where you'd touched me
long sloughed into atmosphere's
swirling *Who?*

That night, standing over the washer's
well, I unknotted sleeves, pants,
bedsheets. I could see
I was going to need a desparate
patience, I could see to get here
they were going to have to take
enormous breaths.

CARETAKERS

Retired, they lived next door.
I'd watch them through the window
over my desk, guessing
what we could turn into
granted leisure with seasons still in it.
She tended flowers;
he, vegetable garden. In the fall
he raked leaves across the yard,
spread newsprint over all the late tomatoes.
She carried armloads of woolens
to the clothesline. Bright October afternoons
I'd watch her
heavy herringbone coat, winter dresses,
his grainy suits
in all the dun colors
of field, dusk
turning on their hangers
this way, that.
in a barely-there wind
as though a ghost of someone they'd loved
tapped, directing attention here,
no, there. Bulk-knit sweaters
would slide to the middle, sinking
as one, and I'd think of scratchiness
airing, its unlikeliness,
of the rash forever rising
beneath my skin, spreading
to scalp, fingers. I once thought
it meant I was allergic to caring
for our surfaces, textures.
I was afraid
and relieved. In November

I watched her bandaging
camellias, re-potting marigolds and coleus
for their kitchen's westerly, lingering
light. He piled pine straw
on top of their borders and bedding.
She called and offered slips
from Joseph's Coat
and Wandering Jew, vines she promised
would flourish
from neglect. If I didn't take them
they'd be left hanging
from the patio roof, abandoned to frostburn,
trailing crisps of old fires.
"I have some," I lied,
almost saying, I keep moths going,
and fieldmice; silverfish; spiders.
But said nothing, knowing the rightness
of her stewardship, the wrongness of my lists
of evasions, the never-cared-for-
enough. I thought to watch her,
him all year, but when Spring came
what with all their rugs drapes windows
rotary tiller seed spreader seeds
and all the birthing world rushing
forward upon us and all that urges after,
I lost track,
what with his already mowing, trimming,
edging, clipping, digging, the small bombs
he planted for rabbits.

MAKING TRACKS

I'm leaving again,
passing through the gate by the cows
heading down the dirt road
with my arms thrown open to air:
I've had such trouble breathing.

I'm going to stake a tent
in the weeds and forget pretending
the house suffers
as we do, that walls weep
over a child's fever, that doors are pleased
when we enter. Goodbye to acquiescence,
that pale ghost that lets dust settle
like slipcovers over bodies.

I know this dirt road by heart,
can smell my way down it by thistle,
ragweed. I know exactly where the doberman
is locked in his pen behind the barn,
exactly how much of his mouth is higher
than fence, exactly the moment my scent
siphons growl
from a deep well in his throat.

This road winds its dusty ellipse
over a path cows must have chosen,
needing endlessness. I know where the road
turns back on itself, where I always lie down
to stare at the sky until it takes my anger.
But this time it's not working:
it's taking longer for fear to whip rage,
to picture the house on the hill
with lamps on at dusk,

the people inside well-fed, leaning
toward happiness like sleep.

It's not fair that a child
always enters this picture,
his face blanched as moonlit field.
Is that what keeps the road
doubling back, having children?
I close my eyes and see you bent,
salvaging tomato plants
from the cutworm's nightly slash
at the base of each stem,
so close to the ground
fingers can't get under,
and I know, No, it's something else,
something. I wonder what happens
in a dog's brain when she's run through fields
all day and starts home,
never thinking, *home,*
only choosing the same door
from so many. A quiet dog, she leaps onto our sofa
and sleeps. We find her on her side,
her legs scooping and shoving air
as if they were still in a field.

GIRL PASSING AMONG TRAILERS

She is maybe eleven, twelve,
though you have to be so young here
not to have had sex
she seems younger.
Thin, barefoot, in yellow shorts
and a blouse loose
as a mother's, a sister's, she walks out
from between two trailers,
crosses the mud-gravel road
toward another trailer,
where someone is calling
or crying. She goes in, comes out
pushing a small child in a stroller.
She maneuvers among loose, bony dogs,
the garbage they've chewed to trash
and scattered across all the yards.
She steers between blankets
where two other girls lie,
blistering, their babies napping fitfully
in a playpen.

It is Spring in the treeless, grass-less
trailer court, though you have to look askance
for signs of urge, surge, prime, burst,
flourish: clumps of dandelion, chickweed
where wheels would be
if these houses moved
as they were meant to; girls oiling
their stretch marks, turning
and turning, as though sun
were all their Spring this year
and from now on.

This is not where each was going
this time last year, when she stared at sky
for all that was about to happen —
the rock music, the boy, the flight
into lives free from parents. At least

that's what they say
to the girl pushing the stroller:
Don't fall for some guy,
Don't get married,
Let us be a lesson,
You'll find out!

I am the cloudy plastic window
she walks past to enter
my daughter's trailer,
saying *Let me, Let me.*
Boil my grandson's water.
Give him a bath, change his diaper.
Changing him, she showers talc
like silk rain
into the folds of flesh,
the creases of tiny arms that reach
to be held, to hold.
She dresses him, cooing, You smell
so good, You so soft, want to go
for a ride? *Let me take him home*
with me, the girl begs my daughter,
who says *not today, my mother doesn't get*
here that often. Bereft, she continues her rounds

in widening concentrics, circling
her shapes of longing
and pleasure through the trailer park
as though straining against her own fullness
of ignorance, bliss.

A POEM FOR SPRING

This morning, when the redbud's clusters
translated into mauve, magenta, the silver maple's
leaves drabbed curls of air
taupish green, and the purple finch
flashed wings the scarlet of fruit
on the black cherry tree, I was afraid.
It was as though,
in other Springs, they'd worn the colors
we named them, but this morning, tugged insistently
as children, urging me close
to something stripped and plain.
All along we've thought it meant something,
these attempts to recognize and label moving parts,
these vigils to catch the world's zillions
becoming; what to call us,
who name most parts wrongly?

The Sunday my sixteen-year-old daughter
told me, "I'm pregnant," we drove two hundred miles
without knowing, and stopped, exhausted,
in Red Boiling Springs, Tennessee,
"where the healing waters flow," the sign read,
"red water, black water, white water."
I gulped tin cups full
and that night we slept in a bed
travelers had come to a century before
for miracle, meaning, *a life different
from this one,* backtracking magic,
deliver us to the beginning.
All the colors of water looked,
tasted the same, metallic and chilled,
each one aching like augury toward places
I'd have root canal, but my daughter chose among them
with care, as though each swallow

mattered. I drove back over tarred ruts
the lame, the dropsical had chosen, and begged
a vision
of each family's heyday:
what could be given,
what could be taken away?

This is a poem about choices,
how when I talk about my daughter,
I can't even say my "small daughter,"
and even that loss has to do
with choice, the one to begin
something inside you
so close
knowing you have chosen
this breaking, this traveling out
this breath
you could never love enough
if not for its leave-taking.

And though I don't know how,
I want it to be a poem about hope,
how this morning, afraid for my daughter, myself,
I called out her name,
"Jenny," the name I gave her, a child myself
in love with cadenzas, coloratura,
nightingales, and all that
lightness, and no one answered
though I called loudly, clearly, again and again
and for a long time.

And nothing matched
what I knew of it,
not even weeds; the nettle we name "red" and
"dead" was first to uncurl its valentine
leaves, first to nudge air with its scallops
of purple; the flax we call "bastard"
and "toad," parasitic, shot chartreuse ellipses,
cups of white sepals so creamy
I soothed my lips with them,

and I turned, looking for hope
where my mother said to look for it,
in ignorance, in mulch, in waste heaps,
in sky the gray
of changelessness, against which, in patches,
barely-there fringiness of leaves
shivered, and a bird, so far away
I couldn't name it, cut
across great distance
to join others, greige agitations
filling a still-bare tree; their chirped,
squawked cacophony reached me
and I translated: *Where are we?*
Where are we going?
Let's stay here! No, farther south!
I'm not moving! Chincoteague marsh!
Live oak, Louisiana! We're hungry, tired.
Hurry!

They were three hills away,
I don't know what they were saying.
Just as I don't know if the hills
were rolling greenness in waves
or I was crying because
the idea of greenness and wings fluttered
so tentatively
there, so up
in the air,
against it.

GOLDFINCHES AT THE NUCLEAR PLANT

You draw me a picture
and ask me to imagine yellow,
black, in undulating
interchange, stripes chopped
from a flag in stiff wind.

But I cannot see
anything, much less birds,
as I walk, before sunrise
from the parking lot down the clay road
following bootprints in the mud
banked up to the Employee Entrance.
Nor can I believe
as the time clock punches
and I file behind others
past sheet rock walls the yellow
of yellow teeth, yellow toenails, yellow snow.

There are no windows here.
I must wait to meet you at lunch
in the field where the cooling tower looms
like a Martian condominium. We break
simple bread under what looks like
simple sky, though complicated with wishing,
waiting, and we stumble onto evidence:
cups of grass, reed strips, spittle,
gold feathers graying into weeds
by the creek bank. It's winter;
goldfinches were here, and are gone.
I imagine one whose feathers I hold
stuttering wings through sky
over Key West, the Gulf, Guatemala,

and as with everything
that doesn't seem to belong,
these winter sunsets like chilled
blackberry currant poured
into white wine, black traceries

of trees like those a welder, in his secret life,
cuts out with scissors so small
they are lost in his hand.

I want to eat the feathers
graft their down onto shoulder blades
or pin them to my hair
as I go back inside the building
after lunch. I want the woman beside me
to look up from her documentation
and think, *flight,*
the man across from me to defect
from technician reports, jump onto his desk,
astonish our air with arm-flapping.

But the feathers stay in my pocket
kept from the woman who limps in
every Monday bruised, welted,
the man with eight mouths beyond his,
all hungry, the supervisor whose wife
has cancer, no insurance,
kept from everyone
who does not belong here

but will lumber, years after I'm gone,
through pre-dawn in steel-toed shoes,
shapes lost inside hooded down,
not thinking
one more month of this,
thinking of migrations
only as moves to new job sites,
dark-to-dark hours everywhere as walls,

as grunt, silence, cold
that enter my pre-waking,
bearing a darkness
like the forever
I have only been a part of.

POEM USING UNUSED LINES

I will begin with "curled maple leaves
shocking gray limbs
with chartreuse" and continue
with "truths people I love
leave me with: I'm always the same distance
from you"; 'Loving means losing';
'When you're lonely, go out and look at the moon.' "
Already, trouble: what do yellow-green leaves,
gray trees have to do with people we love
or distances or moon? Which leads me
to the exercize: I once thought you could connect
any two things
no matter how desperate
the yoking, and if you couldn't,
it was a failure
of the imagination—my son and I
had contests, ironing board/cloud; dinosaur/umbrella;
Byron/chocolate. He always won.
Now if I call the curled maple leaves
a metaphor for hope or
fresh starts or the shock
of new against old, it's but a short step
to words people promise each other,
parting. Or phases of leaves
could be linked
to phases of moon, with human
waxing, waning between
and I could arrive at a poem
about how terribly we miss
the people we love, yet how wise
we're not together
in one room. Or I could call each of us
a soul, alone, that goes out one night

to look at the moon. The soul's
been drinking. It needs air, something distant
to fill with. At such a time
moon could be fleck, wafer, bulb,
it wouldn't matter; the soul
would feel pulled
and respond by imagining its mates,
scattered all over creation
but here tonight, at this moment,
equidistant as memory. Inside this moment
we could say each soul rejoices in the collapse
of reality, nothing wind chill
or its name called from inside the house
wouldn't cure. I don't know. Maybe
a poem using unused lines
should be about the difference
between used and wasted,
though a friend tells me
they're the same, that used up,
he'll describe himself wasted.
But I keep thinking of that man
who jumped into the freezing river
after the plane crashed,
who almost gave his life
to save a stranger, both their lungs
burning blue; now *that* was use.
And I think of my friend who fired a gun
into his throat at thirty-seven.
That was waste. I'd say most of us

fall somewhere between,
more like places by railroad tracks, roadsides
the careless passerby would name
nothing, or weeds. But Roger Tory Peterson
got wall-eyed, he said, crawling
with pencil, sketchpad, capturing wildflowers —
one of each color, each shape.
All night he'd stay up in his motel room

sorting species, variants, mutations.
He had a list of sixty ways to say
a plant is not smooth — words like aculeate, canescent,
hispidulous, pubescent, . . . and still, he said, one leaf
of Vipers Bugloss would fall through
all his phyla, remaining perfectly
indescribable, beauty that could
rip your skin off.

Often we have no say
in what gets used. But tonight
I am thirty-nine years old, choosing
among distances, intent beyond reason
on connections. I'm standing in a yard
in Indiana, looking at the moon.
The C&O clatatraks south beyond
the stripped maples, a blues tenor sax
someone's filled with smoke,
carbon. And though what is anyone
if not a spine
of blue notes, flatted, fretted, vaporizing
toward the memory of music,
I listen. I wait,
letting whatever wants to blow through me
resume its nettling exhalations.

For all I know
it's the amputee
who lived with me one summer,
his good arm spliced to his vanished's
heft and shove, its nearly legible
calligraphy. He's refusing again
my blundering pity, refusing
bursitis draining out the cuff

of his hollow sleeve.
He would reach for me
with nothing,
those whorls of pure intention
and not understand why
I kept washing the dishes.

I belive,
I really do believe
that reach keeps pulsing   out there   somewhere.

I turn, asking, "Yes?"
as it crooks its hapless elbow
around my shoulder.

GLOSSOLALIA

Downstairs, women are speaking
in tongues. I do not understand them,
but as the warbled, garbled syllables rise,
it's just as hard
not to imagine
each tongue's reaching new bars
of music, each head's sputtering lick
of clarifying flame,
as to believe
in the hopelessness of speech
or in atmosphere that bears out words
to blue heavens, where we'll spend eternity
taking them back.

It was just as difficult not to believe
my father was a messenger from God
as to swallow his messages. Aphasiac at the end,
he stammered a language of letting go,
a radical phonics of reconnections,
his tongue breaking
through thickets of loss
to rename the world's parts with absolute
imperfection. When I laid my head
on his chest, I heard a wind
rasping dry leaves, consonants swept like trash,
tracks, trouble from a room I did not want
to lie in,
a room where, years later,
my daughter and I would drop
to our knees in an anguish
of incoherencies, our single agreement
on links between blood,

betrayal, allegiance, judgement, mercy,
children, mothers, screaming
an agreement she never speaks of,
cleaning her house, tending her child.
A covenant like a room swept,
moved out of, words like nail holes   ·
new tenants plaster over
until even the absences inside them are lost.
She could be a woman after my own dumb heart,
now that, more than anything, I want to call her,
tell her how,
when I was eighteen, a boy I loved
was killed; every night for a month
two friends and I lit candles,
balanced a Ouija board on our knees,
asked it questions.
Every night for a month
something answered.
I later thought, *knees, fingers,*
oscillations of brain, heart's throb
for connections.

But if I was wrong,
if they were souls,
they believed in God
but were not with him.
It was dark there, unimaginably crowded,
and lonely.
Call it Robert, John, Martha, father,
sister, lover
it would come
spelling *Yes.*
Anything to hold
attention,

anything not to be
air
or countlessness
of stars, angels.
Hours later I could still feel the graze
of fingertips against the plastic triangle
pulling me down the alphabet,
my true love's leaning like curvature
of time, space, breathing.
Now I think we were calling ahead
to ourselves, *Whither?* and calling back,
Choose me. But if I am wrong

lost souls are more in love
with our voices and hands
than we imagine, and
so lonely that when bored, exhausted
with their world, we'd spell *Goodbye,*
the triangle would slide
out from under our fingers to *No.*

NOT MEETING

A man I love will fly out of Richmond
the day before I arrive.
It's been like this for years —
Pittsburgh, Nashville, St. Louis —
our paths intersecting
without our bodies. There's no
getting used to it; each time I think
there should be something — fluorescence,
clots of glue — where paths cross, re-cross,
until the feet decide
nothing's worth this hurry.

My daughter, when she lived with me,
could stand at a window and sigh
farther than the hills of wild vetch
at the end of our view. I knew
she wanted to be that trail
of breath, heading out on her own
exhalation. I aimed sigh after sigh
to cross hers
in the middle distance, but in the end
all I had was spent breath. I could have stood
between her and the hills, waving red flags,
shouting her name: she wouldn't have noticed.
I can't see vetch now without thinking
of not meeting her,
of the Not
next to everything that is.

Perhaps not meeting keeps us
large, and ghostly. The first time

I went to Boston after a man I loved there
was killed, I just missed him
rounding the corner, descending to the subway.
Today I read of a decomposed body
found in a boxcar: no name, no home, no time,
place, or cause of death.
He'd been rolling in that boxcar
God knows how long. A detective traced it
from Ogden through East St. Louis, Evansville,
Owensboro, to storage, disconnections, repairs
in "remote rural areas . . ."

Packing, I can't get him out of my mind,
not there so long he's lost fingerprints,
second skin on his penis, lips,
the inside of his mouth,
can't stop thinking of the way
absence changes air
into something more biting,
as though there's a special, thin
wind called in for these occasions.

Trying to pack, I see the boy's size 9 sneakers
traveling cross-country for months, not running
into anyone. This makes me so sad
I almost don't want to travel
anywhere, remembering my last arrival
where, instead of one I loved
there was woman with matted, wild hair, lost
in a threadbare Navy peacoat, pacing.

I want to think the foot knows
when it comes to a crossing,
that it shakes off its shoe, treads
barefoot, softly . . .

Landing in Richmond, I'll be wearing a dress
the color of smoke, of almost-absence.
Not meeting me, he'll blow kisses,
calling Paula Paula, across the baggage counter,
the runway, the wings and propeller, through jets
of exhaust, calling Stay there, Stay there,

and the air thins,
slips nearer the bone.